SO-AAZ-862

Best Wishes,

Val Rousseau

My Favorite Beaches

of
Rhode Island and Southeastern Massachusetts

by Valerie Rousseau
Author and Artist

Table of Contents
Page

Horseneck Beach

Westport, Massachusetts

"...surf's up, off to the beach! "

Horseneck Beach

Beautiful Horseneck Beach is noted as one of the BEST beaches in all of New England! Just take Rte. 195 (Ma.) to exit 10 (Rte. 88 Westport, Ma.) and continue south until you cross a little bridge, stay on the left and follow signs to Horseneck Beach...open your windows and enjoy the wonderful scent of the salt air.

Horseneck is a sandy, 2 mile stretch of wonderful beach along the Atlantic Ocean, usually boasting great waves. There is a paved drive that runs along the sand's edge that will be helpful for wheelchairs, carriages, carts and walking.

Hydrangea

The Laughing Gull

Horseneck Beach
Westport, Ma

Protected dunes at Westport Beach....take good
care of them...

Knobbed Whelk

Horseneck Beach,
 Westport, Ma

There are wooden walkways to get from the parking lot, over the protected dunes to the beach. It can be a long hike from your car...so do get there early and you'll have a better chance of getting a parking space nearer an entrance and a great spot on the beach.

There can be an undertow here, as with many open ocean beaches, so just beware...if so, good to stick close to the lifeguard stands, especially if you have children with you.

Horseneck Beach
Westport, Ma

Dial into the posted local radio station on the way down to catch both the surf projections and the parking situation.

Beach Plums

Horseneck Beach
Westport, Ma

Gooseberry Island

Westport, Massachusetts

"let's visit an island..."

Gooseberry Island

Drive past Horseneck Beach and take a right at the very end. Continue over the causeway to Gooseberry Island.

This is a unique experience. There is limited parking on this island (only 50 cars)...but it is well worth the 'early trip' and there is no fee for parking. It's a very natural setting, with footpaths that traverse throughout the landscape...and it's 'dog friendly' but don't forget your leash.

Be advised: there are NO lifeguards here...the north side has a protected beach, but the south side is exposed to the open ocean and can be rough water.

The entire island is covered with beautiful seashore shrubs, trees and plants...a perfect habitat for shorebirds.

It's a wonderful place for sunbathing, painting, picnicking, photography...or just enjoying the natural surroundings.

Very impressive.

Gooseberry Island
Westport, Ma.

11

Knobbed Whelk

Gooseberry Island
Westport, Ma

Piping Plover

Gooseberry Island
Westport, Ma

13

Apponagansett Park
South Dartmouth, Massachusetts

"...let's go to the park today"

Apponagansett Park

Located at 77 Gulf Road in South Dartmouth, Massachusetts...this is a unique sandy beach with great scenic harbor views. It has a nice swimming area, a gazebo you can rent for small functions (you must reserve this in advance), a picnic area, volleyball court, playground equipment and a basketball court. Fun for everyone!

Lifeguards are available during the summer months. There are fees for parking and special events. The water is a protected harbor, so the surf is good for the children. This beach is only a short distance from scenic Padanaram Harbor.

Apponagansett Park
South Dartmouth, Ma

Apponagansett Park
South Dartmouth, Ma

17

Great Blue Heron

Apponagansett Park
South Dartmouth, Ma

Grinnell's Beach
Tiverton, Rhode Island

"...let's go watch the boats go by"

Grinnell's Beach

Located in Tiverton, RI...off Main Road (Rte. 77) is a quaint little beach next to the Stone Bridge Pier.

It's a good spot for the kids...as the surf is usually pretty calm. There is a lifeguard, a children's playground, picnic tables and benches...you can hike/walk or fish....swim or just play in the sand. It has restroom facilities with showers and rooms for changing.

A great bonus with this beach is that if you are in this area, you don't have to drive all the way to the south shore to find a nice little beach, as Grinnell's is about a mile south of the new Sakonnet Bridge in Tiverton.

Grinnell's Beach looks out at the Sakonnet River and Gould Island, in the East Passage of the Mount Hope Bay. The summer brings boat traffic nearby the beach, as they continue by the pier on their way to the harbor, marinas and points north.

Grinnell's Beach
Tiverton, RI

Cormorant

Quahog

Grinnell's Beach
Tiverton, RI

Grinnell's Beach can only accommodate 50 cars, so get there early. Sit back and enjoy. You will find a parking fee during the summer season.

Grinnell's Beach
Tiverton, RI

23

Fogland Beach

Tiverton, Rhode Island

"...maybe we'll see some windsurfers today"

Fogland Beach
Tiverton, Rhode Island

Fogland Beach is in Tiverton, Rhode Island. If you like your beaches a little calmer, I might suggest visiting Fogland Beach in Tiverton. It's a wide, sandy beach on the east side of the Sakonnet River...great for windsurfing and swimming. You can fish nearby and enjoy the beautiful surroundings.

Keep an eye out for wildlife. The river setting is a natural habitat for many species.

Lesser Yellowlegs

Fogland Beach
Tiverton, RI

This is a great place for the children as the beach is upriver and protected. There are lifeguards, changing rooms with showers and even a playground.

Lots of wildlife...parking (for a fee)...picnic tables, restrooms, hiking, windsurfing and fishing! This is a great beach to take a walk. The beach stretches out into the river so you have a wonderful view.

Fogland Beach
Tiverton, RI

26

Windsurfer at Fogland Beach...Tiverton, RI

Fogland Beach
Tiverton, RI

South Shore Beach
Little Compton, RI

"...I love this ocean beach ! Great surf..."

South Shore Beach
Little Compton, RI

After a pleasant ride through Little Compton, (going south on Long Highway), you'll come to the end of South Shore Road...and the Atlantic Ocean. Like a step back in time, you drive onto a large dirt parking lot...and you can actually park adjacent to where you swim.

A large sandy beach wraps around the ocean shore and the offshore view is just great! On a clear day, you can see both Cuttyhunk and the rest of the Elizabeth Islands.

Also...watch out for the nesting Piping Plovers!
Shhhhh...

Piping Plover

South Shore Beach
Little Compton, RI

There is a parking fee for non-residents, but passes are available – weekly or seasonal. You will want to come back!

You'll find lifeguards on duty and portable restrooms. If you take a walk on the beach...going east, you will come to a wildlife refuge known as Goosewing Beach. You have to cross the tidal creek to get there, so be sure to check the incoming tide schedule to ensure your safe return.

On several visits, there have been food vendors, but not a given.

Nautilus Shell

South Shore Beach
Little Compton, RI

South Shore Beach
Little Compton, RI

Sandy Point Beach

Portsmouth, Rhode Island

"...oh...a river beach. Great fun, maybe more birds"

Sandy Point Beach

Located in Portsmouth, RI, on the west side of the Sakonnet River (take Route 138 S/East Main Rd., in Portsmouth...to Sandy Point Avenue on the left).

Here lies a beautiful, peaceful, wide sandy beach about ½ mile long, nestled in quiet residential Portsmouth. The beach offers a small bath house and restrooms. As it's on the river, it's well protected for swimming.

Non-residents will pay to park. The site has picnic tables, benches and a large parking lot with a wooden walkway to the water.

This is a great place to stroll along the shore...watch for the wildlife along the river or just relax and enjoy the surroundings.

Sandy Point Beach
Portsmouth, RI

Great Blue Heron

Sanderling

Sandy Point Beach
Portsmouth, RI

Kill Deer

Sandy Point Beach
Portsmouth, RI

Third Beach
Middletown, Rhode Island

"...I really love this beach...let's go"

Third Beach

A great place to enjoy a summer's day. A wonderful sandy beach at the mouth of the Sakonnet River where it meets the Atlantic, offering a little more protection from the southerly ocean breeze.

You can enjoy watching the small boats (18 feet and under) as they come and go...they are allowed to drop anchor right off shore. There is a boat ramp available and the swimming areas are clearly marked for your protection.

Third Beach
Middletown, RI

Nearby (583 Third Beach Road) you will find the
Norman Bird Sanctuary...lots of trails wind through
meadows and marshlands where they meet the
Sakonnet River and the beach.

Third Beach
Middletown, RI

The Sanctuary has a gift shop and museum...with lots of information...a great place to visit. It offers walking trails across the fields and wetlands...where you can observe the wildlife. This is a wonderful spot for photography or a great place to get out that sketch pad or just enjoy Mother Nature.

The coastal ecosystems provide a habitat for lots of wildlife throughout the entire year and the views are well worth the trip.

Norman Bird Sanctuary

Third Beach and Norman Bird Sanctuary
Middletown, RI

Herring Gull

To enjoy Third Beach, take Third Beach Road to the
very end and you will find parking with seasonal
fees...

Third Beach
Middletown, RI

Second Beach

Middletown, Rhode Island

"...I'm so excited; we are going to Second Beach, one of my very favorites..."

Second Beach

You have to visit Second Beach in Middletown! It's right on the Atlantic Ocean, off Sachuest Point Road. It's wide and runs about a mile and a half...along the shore. Yes, yes...lots of people in the summer, so get there early and enjoy!

Sanderlling

What's there to do at Second Beach ??
Lots: Swimming...Playing in the surf...Playing in
the sand...Walking...Surfing...Sunbathing.

There's plenty of parking, a concession stand,
lifeguards, restrooms, changing rooms and picnic
tables.

Second Beach
Middletown, RI

Easton's Beach -
First Beach in Newport, RI

"...yes, yes. Let's go to First Beach..."

First Beach

A great beach for the entire family...next to Cliff Walk in Historic Newport, Rhode Island. This beautiful sandy beach looks out on the Atlantic Ocean with lots of amenities for everyone. It includes a carousel, amusements, skateboarding area and a cement boardwalk that runs the length of the beach with picnic tables and benches. Of course there is great sand and lots of waves.

Easton's (First) Beach
Newport, RI

There are lifeguards, restrooms, showers and rental bathhouses...and a great snack bar.

Quahog

Easton's Beach
Newport, RI

Narragansett Town Beach

Narragansett, Rhode Island

"...we're off to South County and Narragansett"

Narragansett Town Beach

Great town beach! Take scenic 1-A Rhode Island, driving south. You will come to a beautiful, wide sandy beach...for your pleasure.

Swimming, walking, sunbathing, kayaking, surfing, etc. etc., with lots of parking.

Narragansett Town Beach
Narragansett, RI

This is an impressive beach....there are both beach
pavilions and changing rooms available for a rental
fee.

Narragansett Town Beach
Narragansett, RI

There are lots of places to eat, public restrooms and great little shops all nearby.

Narragansett Town Beach
Narragansett, RI

Parking for a fee...lots of town programs available during the summer months. Lifeguards are on duty.

Narragansett Town Beach
Narragansett, RI

Scarborough State Beach

Narragansett, Rhode Island

"...can't wait to show you Scarborough Beach. I know you will love this one..."

55

Scarborough State Beach

One of Rhode Island's most popular beaches –
beautiful, with shade-providing gazebos, picnic areas,
benches and a great wooden boardwalk.

A wide, sandy beach...perfect for swimming or just
walking along the shore. Follow Rhode Island 1-A
south to Narragansett.

Scarborough State Beach
Narragansett, RI

Scarborough Beach offers lifeguards, concession stands, changing facilities, restrooms and showers.

It's a wonderful beach and one of Rhode Island's most popular. It offers gazebos for shade and picnic areas.

Scarborough State Beach
Narragansett, RI

You will find plenty of parking – access from Ocean Road, (fee to park) and large grassy playing fields right across the street (Scarborough South Side).

A must-see beach you are sure to love.

Scarborough State Beach
Narragansett, R

Roger Wheeler State Beach
(Sand Hill Cove Beach)
Narragansett, Rhode Island

"...yes, let's bring the family to this great beach..."

Sand Hill Cove Beach, Roger Wheeler State Beach

Also known as Sand Hill Cove Beach to the locals, a great family beach...at the end of Sand Hill Cove Road, west of Point Judith. An ocean beach that is protected by several breakwaters...making it a great beach with calm waters...just perfect for swimming and the whole family.

Drive south in Narragansett and you will find this beach at the east end of Sand Hill Cove Road. Lots of great restaurants nearby too.

Check out the Pt. Judith Light (before you get to the beach...follow Ocean Road all the way south).

Sand Hill Cove Beach
Narragansett, RI

Roger Wheeler beach offers lifeguards, picnic areas and food concessions...a great playground for children...with restrooms and changing facilities...has handicap access. Great sandy beach with lots of space.

Herring Gull

Sand Hill Cove Beach
Narragansett, RI

"Thanks for coming to the beach with me. Have fun, find your own favorites and don't forget the sunscreen!"

"...bye for now"

This book is dedicated to my loving Mom...whose lifelong dedication to creating art both inspired me and taught me to appreciate the beauty that surrounds us all.

Val Rousseau

About the Author and Artist:

Valerie Rousseau is a local Rhode Island artist, a member of the Portsmouth Arts Guild and the Bristol Art Museum. She shows at several local galleries and graduated from the University of Massachusetts and studied at Rhode Island School of Design.

All paintings and drawings are the original work of the artist. No portion of this book may be reproduced without the written permission of the author.

This book is not intended to be a legal document, but thoughts, opinions and observations of the artist.

Copyright by the author of this book. The book author retains sole copyright to her contributions to this book.